NATIONAL GEOGRAPHIC

T0045224

Make a Piñata!

Michelle Freeman

We are going to make a piñata.
We need all of these things.

bowl
water
spoon
PLAIN
FLOUR
flour
tape
balloons
crepe paper
glitter

First, we blow up a balloon.

Next, we mix flour and water to make a paste.

Then, we tear newspaper into strips.

We dip each newspaper strip in the paste.

Next, we cover the balloon with the wet newspaper strips.

We wrap two long pieces of string around the balloon so we can hang it.

Then, we cover the balloon with more wet newspaper strips.

We let the newspaper strips dry overnight.

In the morning, we pop the balloon and pull it out of the piñata.

Then, we fill the piñata with candy and close the opening with tape.

Next, we paint the piñata to look like a fish.

We add crepe paper fins and put glitter on the scales.

Who can break the piñata?